KNOWLEDGE CUBE CONCEPT

Ignite Your Passion to Become Successful

ANDREW CM MILLER

WOW Book Publishing™

First Edition Published by Andrew CM Miller

WOW Book Publishing™

ISBN: 978-1-09-192269-3

The purpose of this book is to educate and entertain. The views and opinions expressed in this book are that of the author based on her personal experiences and education. The author does not guarantee that anyone following the techniques, suggestions, ideas or strategies will become successful.

The author shall neither be liable nor responsible for any loss or damage allegedly arising from any information or suggestion in this book.

Dedication

I wrote this book to reach out to you and to help you to re-ignite that 'flame' within you.

I dedicate this book to you to spark the interest in you that you once had. I want to remind you that: 'Who you are and what you do will determine your successes.'

To your success,

Andrew CM Miller
Your Transitional Coach

Contents

Testimonials

Andrew has help me start my life all over again, giving me new perspective on life. He has helped others and me in achieving our goals. I recommend him to anyone who needs assistance in finding their path to success.

—Yaneak Phillips
Administrative Assistant
New York, USA

Due to Andrew's years of dedication and commitment to working with young people, he shares his wealth of knowledge and experience throughout this personal development book *The Knowledge Cube Concept.* You will find his writing encouraging, inspiring, and energizing.

—Sam Beaumont
Mentoring Project Officer
London, UK

With his knowledge and experience, Andrew has demonstrated his leadership and motivational qualities. His book, *The Knowledge Cube Concept,* will break down some key component of the Mastermind principles that will be food for your personal growth.

—Odingo Jackson
Specialist Nanny
Executive at Kimona Maternity Services
Kent, UK

I met Andrew during his early rise of becoming a New Professional. As a well committed student at CUNY: College, he became an independent business owner in Network Marketing. Andrew has achieved a milestone of putting together from his wealth of experiences and Personal Development much-needed content to help you in his book, *The Knowledge Cube Concept.* I recommend Andrew as the go-to person to assist you on your success journey.

—Paul Mortimer
Independent Consultant
Staten Island, USA

Andrew has been passionate for some years about *the knowledge cube.* He has been using his ideas to inspire others to 'pick themselves up again' and has helped me look at the importance of my health and wellbeing through which I continue to dedicate time to my physical fitness. I know Andrew's book, *The Knowledge Cube Concept*, will give you an inside view of how you too can revive your interest and live life more fully.

—Elaine Smith
Health Care Support Worker
London, UK

Andrew has given me inspiration and motivation to achieve my goals. He has made it possible for me to dream again. I want to recommend him as the go-to person to revive your interest and relive your dreams.

—Rocshelle Rock-Miller
Early years Educator
Day Nursery Proprietor
London, UK

About the Author

Andrew wrote this book to inspire you. He wants to help spark any interest you desire to have or to reignite what you once had toward achieving success at something—anything.

He has developed through his own leadership training and personal development and guidance gained from accessing continuous mentoring. Andrew had a range of transitional experiences working in Network Marketing and working within the Education, Social Care, and Health Care industries. His discipline also encompasses his military training and commitments.

Andrew has expanded his knowledge base, skills, and education while growing up in the Caribbean, emigrating to the USA, and later, settling in the United Kingdom. He continues to align himself with professionals and attends workshops to sustain a current mindset.

He finds interest in helping people achieve their dreams and aspirations and reach their true potential.

Foreword

Dear Reader,

***The Knowledge Cube Concept** is the book you need to read to learn more about returning some vigour to what you once believed in and to ignite some flame within yourself.*

Andrew has identified and moulds the power of masterminding. He imparts it in a way that will allow you to spark that flame within you and take that necessary action.

The information in this book has the power to help you recreate the lifestyle you deserve and that which you desire. I can relate to some of the teachings, ideas, and practices in this book.

I can tell you from my interaction with Andrew that he is filled with a wealth of life skills experiences and he has the willingness to help you achieve your goals in a powerful way.

—Vishal Morjaria
International Speaker
Award Winning Author

Acknowledgements

I acknowledge the impact of some who created a path for me who have passed on, such as Napolcon Hill, Stephen Covey, and Mr Cyprian Miller. I wish to express my deepest appreciation to the WOW Book team, including the beautiful Book Angels who journeyed with me at the end to make this real. I would say thank you Vishal Morjaria for helping to bring this book out from within me.

My gratitude goes out to all who have been part of an establishment that worked with me on this path, especially at Missionaries of the Poor (Kingston-Jamaica)', Medgar Evers College (CUNY), SCCD (London), the Youngevity & Escape International leadership, the Salvation Army-Social Care services (UK), the MoD (UK), the Internet Business School, and the Master Coach team.

I am grateful for the support of my extended family members. I wish to thank and highlight the support of members of 'the Knowledge Cube's Circle,' Odingo Jackson, Adonis Claude Miller, and young Research Specialist and student Malik John.

I acknowledge some of the great influential contributors to my huge learning journey: Sir Richard Branson, Robert Kiyosaki, Earl Nightingale, and Rob Moore as well as those

I have had direct communication with like Dr Joel D. Wallach, Tom Chenault, T. Harv Eker, Les Brown, Anthony Robbins, Andy Harrington, and Paul O' Mahony.

I acknowledge my friends, colleagues, and supporters of this book for believing in me.

I acknowledge the divine and highest power for my strength and sense of discernment.

Finally, I acknowledge you for receiving and using this book to add value to your life and I thank you for taking action today.

Note to the Reader

The information, including concepts, opinions, and instructions it contains is based on the author's personal experiences and views and is not intended to provide exclusive professional advice.

The author and the publisher make no warranties, expressed or implied, relating to accuracy, applicability, effectiveness, reliability, or suitability of the contents. If you wish to apply or follow the advice or recommendations mentioned herein, you take full responsibility for your actions. The author and publisher of this book shall in no event be held liable for any direct, indirect, incidental, or consequential damages arising from the use of any of the information contained in this book.

All content is for information only and is not warranted for content accuracy or any other implied or explicit purpose.

CHAPTER 1
YOUR PASSION

HOW I CAN HELP YOU FIND YOUR PASSION

I can help you achieve anything that you want to achieve. Now, before we explore this further, I must tell you that someone has tried their best to debate this fact with me, to question me, and to challenge me about this reality. Others have even tried to dispute this with the explanation that I can't make them do anything. My response to them, and to you here now, is that I can help you achieve anything you want to achieve.

When you want to achieve something, I actually guide you. It's as if I hold your hand and lead you on your path from the front. You simply have to follow, but it's actually your path that you told me you want to be on. In this sense, I lead you toward your path. But what I actually do is help you to create within yourself that hunger, that need, that strong desire, that feeling of warmth and joy within yourself that makes you want to achieve and succeed.

Have you ever asked yourself, "How hungry am I to achieve my goal?" It's important to ask the questions. How hungry are you? How much do you really want this? How will it make you feel once you have achieved this? How will you feel if you don't achieve this goal? What will happen after you achieve this goal?

Often, we are overjoyed by simple, witty posts, whether on social media, in face to face interactions, or shared with us on television screens and on our computers and other devices. Yet we cannot find laughter in what we're actually trying to achieve. Why not consider channelling your energies in a more direct form, in a more possible form, and in a more eventful form?

MY EXPERIENCE FINDING MY OWN PASSION

I am a very passionate person about many things. But that passion did not come naturally. I like nature. I like and admire people who have fun. And I like driving. These are areas I'm very passionate about, for several reasons.

My admiration for nature is deep-rooted as I grew up around white sand beaches in the Caribbean. I continued to explore and enjoy nature and the tropical feeling internationally, before emigrating to the United States of America. I had some of my first American life experiences in Florida before going to New York. There, my enthusiasm increased with my interest in what the suburb areas of Brooklyn and the metro areas in Queens was like.

In New York City, I developed a new passion for nature, especially in places like Prospect Park where I lived. And the busy-ness, the rustling, and the environment helped to channel my energies and my focus and to achieve. While everything and everyone around me was mostly busy and rushed about, I was able to visit the park and enjoy a little of nature. I took time out for the trees, small creatures and plants, and especially, the birds and the squirrels.

When I had the opportunity to get close to the coast, or at those times when I would go to the river views of Manhattan, I was able to reflect better on my upbringing and my experiences of the Caribbean. Once I migrated to the United Kingdom, I was then surrounded with the wealth of greenery, parks, rivers, and the peace and calm of the river rides.

My passion is something that grew outwards. I developed a drive within myself and became more and more passionate about what I did and what I enjoyed. I no longer liked the fastest cars in life and instead, I somehow enjoyed the whole new perspective of being able to drive in such a different environment. All the busy-ness seemed different. Then I learned more and more about the underground, over-ground, DLR, the transport network, the national rail, and how easy it was to get around in such a busy environment. All this discovery made me excited, and I believe that this is what passion does for you. It gets you excited.

So every time I feel my excitement, it reminds me of how passionate I was or am today. My passion grew in the need and desire to help people. Perhaps this was my 'why' for working in the healthcare industry as a healthcare practitioner or working in the social care sector as a project worker. Perhaps it was my 'why' for working as a teaching assistant in the education sector.

I enjoyed what I did. I engrossed myself in what I did and my services in helping others achieve their dreams. And since then, while building and developing the Knowledge

Cube system and concept, I continually grew in my passion and my love for what I did and what I do today.

THE POWER OF PASSION

Have you ever had that strong desire of wanting something or wanting to achieve something? That overwhelming feeling of why you want to do what you're about to do?

When you have a strong desire for something—a goal, a target, or that thing you want to achieve—it creates a type of adrenalin. I may not be able to explain it from a professional standpoint, but I can definitely say that I, too, have experienced this increase in strength, in power, and in might. That increase in drive to want to go after my goal and my dreams.

When you really desire your goal, when you really feel like you can achieve your dream, there is nothing stopping you. The strength you develop, the might you gain, and the action you take, become a very positive force that you can call your power.

The power of your passion is like having a hunger or appetite for a particular food that you particularly love. When you see that food, you smell it and inhale the spices and the vigour. It's as if you've already enjoyed that food or that dish. The same applies for your favourite drink, about being thirsty and about to quench your thirst. When you first touch the glass or the bottle, it's as if you already have it and have taken it in. This extra strength, this extra drive, this extra feeling, all come from the power of passion.

Very often, I think that when we meet or connect with that which we're about to achieve—or what we really want to achieve—we tend to develop an inner strength or inner drive. Consider an athlete, the fastest man at this time, Usain Bolt. If you look at a video of when he wants to win or when he is winning and slow it down, you are able to clearly see the expression on his face, the gritting of his teeth, his muscles, and his strides. He develops an extreme and powerful strength as he envisions the finish line, that gold medal, and that roar of the crowd. That's what I like to think is the power of passion.

WHAT ARE YOU PASSIONATE ABOUT?

When you feel good about something—you know, like really good—you tend to move, react, think, and act as if it's natural and sometimes supernatural, type of behaviour and action. So what is it that you're really passionate about? When you have given it enough thought, does it really resonate with you? Or do you feel like you are developing a larger drive or an excitement or desire to do it? Why not simply say something about it right now? Perhaps you want to shout it out or express it to someone or in some way?

Now that you have found that one thing—that idea or thought—feel it. Really appreciate and feel it. Let it consume you and take over your feelings, right now. After all, it's your feelings, your ideas, and your passion. Now, keep it with you. Later on, I will explore this passion so keep it there with you.

Do you find it quite difficult to uncover that desire, that drive, or that thing that you want to achieve? That inspiration! The passion comes from wanting to really experience and be revved up by something. So it definitely comes with your desires, what you want to achieve, and what you want to gain.

I can't tell you what this is, so it will definitely need your effort. This is especially true if you're not sure what you're passionate about or what you want to achieve now or in the future. Let's start an exercise today. I challenge you, I dare you, and I will support you in your action task today.

Take at least fifteen minutes only. Find a quiet place. It can be early in the morning or in the evening, but take this quiet moment where perhaps it's dark and sit or relax wherever you feel comfortable. But don't lie down. You may fall asleep while doing this. Take this time out to explore something that you feel strongly about in your own mind. Something that you desire.

After this fifteen minutes, why not write it down? Write it down and leave it there, and we'll come back to it later. We will also explore this a little further as you read on because it could actually be a daily activity that you start practising today.

WHY DO YOU NEED PASSION?

We all need to have passion if we're excited about achieving something or at least about something or someone we love. If it's something we want to achieve or to experience, we must have this strong desire within ourselves to achieve it or we simply won't accomplish it. At least, not any time soon.

Previously, you examined your passions. In fact, I helped you to think and feel something which, you could say, is one thing that you are passionate about. Did you feel that drive? Did you reach that level of excitement? Did you come up with an idea or something you want to achieve? Do you want to propel or more importantly, want to move, act, or do something about it? We need passion to help our excitement, to increase our energy levels or our adrenalin, and to increase and develop that drive within us that will push us forward.

In fact, all successful people I have met are passionate about something or have been passionate about what they've achieved. They have a strong desire that makes them want to act, perform, or succeed. This desire kept them training, practising, seeking improvement, and seeking that level of excellence to perform. When the day comes, or when that event or activity comes, you must be ready! It can be a test or even an exam. It could be a workshop, somewhere you have to be where you have to express yourself and let people examine you or critique you. Perhaps it's something that puts you into the limelight or puts you out there, where all you have around you is what I call cheerleaders—those who will cheer you on or others who will simply get excited.

If you're not yet excited or inspired about your idea, something particular that you want to achieve, remember that with passion, you too can succeed. You can develop an unstoppable drive within you that makes you want to move. We all need this feeling to get us out of our snobbish modes or our depressing feelings and to enable us to move and maintain that motion. I can help you find this passion. I could help develop you and your drive if you'll only join with me. If you haven't done it before, have a go at it. Find that thing that you're passionate about.

As I think of my own personal development, one of the things I learned from one of the early fathers of personal development, Earl Nightingale, comes to mind. He stated that we must have a strong desire to achieve that which we go after. If we don't have that strong desire, we'll be out of energy, we'll be slow, dragging our feet, and taking our good old time. We will, quite simply, be late.

Sometimes, I think of my own time at school and even at college, where I'd get to class late. I can recall that I'd been at school all day, every day, and on that particular day, they wanted me to do the same thing once again. I had no interest. I had to go to class only because I had to. But what if you actually go into that session and you love it to the degree where, let's say, you're completely passionate about learning and about what you go there for? Perhaps it's your best class, your best subject.

Do you see the difference? That if it's something that you care about and which you want to do, you then go out of love and desire for it and will be full of excitement. You'll go after it, full of energy. Is it not that passion, that strong desire within you that keeps you so excited? And that's what we are exploring here today.

WHY YOU NEED PASSION TO BE SUCCESSFUL

Can you imagine standing there and achieving what you want to achieve? Or standing where you are right now and winning a race without putting any effort into it? Can you imagine winning in a car race and not having a car to drive? What about running in brand new trainers without first putting them on? Can you imagine enjoying a dish—your favourite dish—without actually eating it or consuming any part of it?

Consider this: the end results of your simple forms of success lie within your imagination. You need to have a hunger, a need, a want, or a desire. In this instance, I call it passion. And you need to act on it in order to succeed at even these small things. Imagine wanting to enjoy your dish and you don't feel it. You're not in the mood. But you want it. So how will you enjoy it if you only want it? Can you imagine, at this stage, that you focus on a goal but on succeeding and achieving it without wanting to take action? Can you imagine not being hungry but merely wanting to eat? Of course you can. However, what would the experience be like?

I remember the 2018 world cup sessions. We saw flags and excitement amongst people. It's as if they, themselves, were involved in playing or participating in the world cup on the pitch or on the football grounds—the excitement, the hunger, and that elated feeling were present. They created within themselves this passion that I refer to. Because they wanted success for the team, they were in this new mood, this new life experience, and this new feeling of belonging.

And with passion, you often experience a new feeling of belonging to, and of wanting to. It draws a sense of energy, excitement, and support from others. When you like something, you love someone, or you're interested in achieving, there's a need for you to be overjoyed with excitement. This makes you feel as if you have already reached your goal and are successful. This feeling is that passion that you need to get to the end and to achieve success.

REFLECTIVE NOTES

Identify one message I received from this chapter:

How does this make me feel?

Who will I speak with to assist me?

What actions can I take right now?

Go to – **www.TheKnowledgeCube.info**—*to discover more*

CHAPTER 2
YOUR WHY, YOUR SUCCESS

ALL WINNERS HAVE A REASON WHY

In my personal development journey, I wanted to achieve. I needed to become a master. I needed to become a professional and I needed to establish a reason for wanting to do this. And on this journey, I met someone whom I consider one of my first or early mentors, Paul, who not only warned me but taught me something specifically that I'll never forget. He said, "Andrew, why do you think winners win?"

Of course, I smiled, and I wanted to laugh. When he looked at me, the expression on his face did not change and he asked me again, "Why do you think all winners win?"

I wanted to say, "Because they're winners." But I knew this was not a productive answer. I looked at him and, of course, I said, "I don't know."

He said, "Well, all winners have a strong reason why they want to achieve. All winners establish a reason for their accomplishment early in their life. It may not be the exact achievement that they gain, but very often, it's much higher." It's a much higher achievement. Why? Because they shoot for the best, for the top. They train, they practise, and they hurt. They nurture their bodies well. And they fight. They fight the pain. They don't slump into depression or boredom.

They don't become sluggish or become ill due to depression and stress and worry. They become almost like super-humans because they leave the worry behind and they set their targets. They set their purpose in life. They say: 'I want to achieve this because—' And that 'because' is their 'why.'

"And if winners have a reason why, should you not also have a reason why?" Paul then said, "You call me your mentor but, Andrew, the reason why I do what I do is not only because I love it. Of course, I love helping people. I love seeing other people achieve their dreams. But I, too, have my reasons why. And would you not say that I am also a winner?"

I learnt that all winners have a reason why. They have a 'because.' They have a 'what.' They have a target. They have something they want to achieve. And they want to achieve well.

So consider this: If all winners have a reason why, would you agree that in order to succeed, you too need to have a reason why?

DO YOU NEED TO HAVE A REASON WHY?

Imagine you get up one morning, step out of bed, probably go to the bathroom, and then go back to bed? What's wrong with this action? Is there anything really wrong with this? After all, there's nothing else you have to do. But what if you have to go to school or to college? Or go to work, to a job? You may need to have a shower and eat something—maybe breakfast cereal, maybe milk, or maybe a hard-core breakfast, a full-blown 'English-style' breakfast. You know, a nice little fry-up. Consequently, you will start preparing because you have somewhere to go.

If it's work, you know you have to get there at a particular time so you have to leave at a particular time. You may have to take public transport or you may drive. Perhaps you may need to have your parents or someone else give you a ride. How will you get there? Why are you actually going there?

Quite simply, I know why you need to have a reason why. I know that without a reason why, there's no need for you to take any particular action. There's no need for you to do anything specific. You can merely stay in bed. You could keep doing what you are doing and, as some people would say, keep on keeping on. There would be no need to divert and no need to deviate in any specific manner.

Your reason why is like your pilot—the guide in front of the aircraft that you might not see but who controls everything else. Your pilot propels your motor or aircraft forward and he or she takes you in the direction of or to that place where you want to go. Even so, whether it's getting from place to place, achieving a particular goal, or obtaining a particular award, we all need purpose in life—purpose to do something, to do anything. To do what we're trying to achieve. And this is why you need to have a reason why. You need purpose. You need to find or establish the, 'what am I doing?' or 'what for?'

HOW TO FIND YOUR WHY

How to find your 'why', as we previously established, is to look at a reason for this thing you want to achieve or want to do. Going back to the earlier examples, we can consider that we need to find a desire. And that the things we want to achieve might be huge. Perhaps we might not be able to see it in our mind's eye right now. However, it's there. Because it's there and you're here, it's sometimes challenging to see it. But this is what we have to do. We have to use imagery to see it or to visualise it.

Think of a foundation, a base for a building. Imagine that there is a cleared plot of land in front of you in your area. You want to build a house. But how do you get this house you want to build there? You have to take things in steps and stages. Move from one to two, to three, to four, and so on. You will, therefore, first need to consider where to start.

Now remember, we want to build a particular house on that plot of land we have. We may need to go to different people in authority or in charge of various processes. We have to get them involved, which means we need to take action. Bearing in mind what it is we want to achieve, the actions that we take are what we will regard as the necessary things to do to get this house built. They are required to get this project to start and to move us toward achieving what we want.

You may not be able to do everything in a very practical way. You may have to take some time out to consider what you want this house or this project to be. What do you want it to look like? You might take some time out and simply think about it, to imagine it as if it's built or is already off the ground. How many bedrooms and how many bathrooms do you want to have? Do you want a driveway? Do you want more than one garage? Where do you want the entrance and the doors?

You can think of this and imagine it, but there are also people who can help you with all this. It might be an architect or an engineer, but you want to look for the person who is qualified in this area and has the expertise. Then, you get them involved so you don't always have to do everything. You don't have to achieve anything on your own.

With the Knowledge Cube, you will see that there are alternative routes. We find the best and most effective way. We help you mould that thing you want to achieve so you can see your reason why for yourself. You will imagine what it is you want and what it looks like. What it is you want and what it feels like. And what you want it to be and want it to contain.

This creates a hunger and a desire that makes you want to propel yourself, to find your drive, to move forward. Finding your reason why, or how to find your reason why, requires some imagery. It involves some soul searching at times—looking inside you and within yourself.

MY 'WHY' EXPERIENCE

My 'why' experience has been quite a journey. Almost everything I've achieved in my life has had a mentor or coach attached to it, although it may not have been from the initial stage. However, when I failed or 'learnt' from not achieving the goal, I attempted it again. And, even though I tried again, it was more than likely with the assistance of someone to guide me, someone who had achieved something similar or in that particular field.

The one crucial thing I know that I've learned in all these experiences and my achievements is that there are times of struggle. Those times when I struggled most were when I did not pay attention to what my coach or mentor told me or simply when I didn't have one. When I did have a mentor or coach, or when I succeeded, the one common question they asked all the time was, "Andrew, why are you doing this? What is your reason why?"

It dawned on me that every time I tried to achieve something, the same question kept coming up: '*My reason why.*' My 'reason why' question came up for the first time when I entered network marketing. I was in New York City. Yes! In the United States of America. I had met one of the first persons I could truly consider my mentor, Paul Mortimer. He was also a professor in one of the 'sister' colleges.

I made mention of Paul because, as a mentor, he was dedicated to me and what I did. One of the things that I realised was that the more I committed I was and I did what I was told, or I followed the process, the more he was there for me—the more he committed as my mentor and the more I achieved. I would say that Paul did help me get on a new path in my life journey and experiences. My personal development process, my reading and development process, my rhythm, and the Knowledge Cube, all started with Paul. He directed me to the right books, gave me the right guidance, and supported me on my journey as a coach and mentor should.

Paul and I did take different paths as I left the USA and continued my process of success in the United Kingdom. However, every time I touch base with him or catch up on what Paul is involved with, he continues to progress in whatever he's doing. He, too, has a strong reason why.

Now that I'm on this new journey and with my book, a new mentor was needed. This book—as this is my first book—was in the making over several years. It was in meeting Vishal and following exactly what he said, following his process, and following his guidance, that I was able to produce this content and continue and excel with the Knowledge Cube process.

I always needed to refer to my reason why and I needed to make my reason why strong enough. And because of my experience and my journey of having to refer to my reason why, I insist that you, too, consider referring back to your reason why.

USING YOUR 'WHY' TO CREATE YOUR SUCCESS

What is your purpose? Yes, you! What is your purpose? Not your purpose in life but your purpose in your desire to achieve your goal. We've established that having a reason why is your 'because,' it's your target, and it's your 'what.' And if we focus on this 'what,' this 'because,' you too must have some tasks or some actions you need to take.

With your reason why, you are bound to succeed if you take the necessary actions. As it is known, an object in motion stays in motion (Newton's law). So too, an action acted upon will increase your results. When you first start to take action, you will continue to propel or move forward. You will continue until you succeed. It doesn't matter what you're actually trying to succeed in right now. Taking action based on your 'because,'—on your target or your reason why—will propel you to exceed your expectations. To exceed your actions, exceed your motion.

Let's establish your 'why,' in particular. And at the end of this chapter, you can use the notes section to recreate or revisit 'your reason why.' Using imagery, let's take steps through your thought process and nurture that imagery through exploring it. Using your posture and your hands to get a sense of feeling of this thought process, your reason why, your 'because,' can be discovered.

With this in mind, we will mould what we want to achieve and take action—to move in a direction forward or upward but toward your success and your goal, toward your target. When we take our first step, our first movement, and then remain in motion, the only thing that matters is our success, our actions, our achievement, and our goal.

WHAT IS YOUR REASON WHY?

Have you decided on any particular reason why you want to do what you're doing right now? Have you given it thought? Have you considered what's important to you? What are you doing it for? Your reason why is made up of a number of personal feelings, things you want to achieve, personal views, and things like that. Your reason why needs to be strong. It needs to be personal to you and it needs to be the reason why you choose to do this thing. Your reason why is a starting point. It was developed because you had a strong feeling that you wanted to do this thing because of something.

Imagine being broke. You have no money, you have bills to pay, and you want a job. It's a low-paying job, but you need a job right now. Because you have bills to pay, you'll take this job. In this instance, your reason why could simply be because you need money and need it right now. You therefore take the job because you need to satisfy a purpose. Hence, your desire becomes real. I need cash so I get the job. I get a job because I need cash. This is a very simple way to put this.

Very often, you set bigger goals. For example, if you are into athletics, you want to win a race and to win trophies. That may be your reason why you start training, start practising, and imagine achieving. Now, consider this as your reason why. You want to win trophies, you want to win medals. You now move to another starting point where you have to train. You have to go to practise sessions, weight training, exercising, and perhaps some cycling. If necessary, maybe start swimming. But you want to be active.

In the same way, this works for any type of goals you want to achieve. Imagine you want to be successful right now at school, in your classroom. You can pick a subject area. Let's simply say you want to improve your maths. You will now start looking at keeping the television off more and staying off your phone or screen devices. Simply dedicate some time in which you can practise, study, and prepare for your tests and assignments. In this way, you're bound to improve.

Of course, you might need some guidance. You can call a coach for now or a friend, a buddy, or someone you're comfortable around. You often can't be accountable to yourself because when you let yourself down, it's very difficult to rebuke or to scold yourself. So, yes, you find someone you're comfortable with but also someone you're already committed to. And commit to yourself: I will do this; I will do this by this time. And you try to do it. You try to do it and you achieve it. Then you achieve it and you do it. When you slip up, you can go to that person. You can have a nice little chat for feedback. We call that person the coach.

Now that your reason why is simple, imagine that you want to pass maths. Now, look at the process. So, as I said before, your reason why is the starting point that gives you that driving force and makes you want to take that step.

REFLECTIVE NOTES

Identify one message I received from this chapter:

How does this make me feel?

Who will I speak with to assist me?

What actions can I take right now?

Go to – **www.TheKnowledgeCube.info**—*to discover more*

CHAPTER 3
THE KNOWLEDGE CUBE

HOW THE KNOWLEDGE CUBE CHANGED ME

Interestingly, when I came up with the idea of the Knowledge Cube and after my first session working in a life house in the health and social care sector, I wasn't a presenter as such. But it opened my interest in reading and learning to know more and to be more of a leader. I began to develop an interesting habit.

Yes, I'd been guided in the past about reading and how to read, what best books to read, and how not to read. Also, how to gain knowledge and how to share and express what I'd learned. After this, I created a habit—a simple habit and system of how to read. It's important, at this time, to recognise that reading was not a favourite thing for me. I didn't enjoy it at the time, but I started getting into it. I developed a process and habit of reading while commuting on buses, trains, and the underground in the city of London, United Kingdom. I took this habit with me while flying between the continents and especially flying between New York City and London, and throughout the other territories that I visit.

Using that as a foundation, I shaped this system for my reading and how to maintain consistency. This was the 'how to' develop my reading and the 'how to' get better at retaining and gaining knowledge and expressing what I'd read. I decide to share it with others—with some of the guys whom I worked with and other colleagues. As a result, I began to gather materials and put structures together. I developed a system of how I could deliver what I'd gained and what I had learnt, encircled by the Knowledge Cube system.

Since that process started well over ten years ago, I have grown through relationships, different environments, moving houses, working in different business sectors, having different jobs, and undergoing different training. Now, consider the fact that the Knowledge Cube system has continued to be there by my side. It is one of those reliable things that remain with me.

When I think of the Knowledge Cube, I think that I'm in my own place, a different place in my head. I felt purposeful and it allowed me to create an imaginary place or an imaginary environment. One filled with peace and tranquillity and that became powerful and colourful. Additionally, it developed an amazing feeling that stayed with me, especially during my low periods.

There are times in anyone's experience in life and in growing up when you will have highs and lows. When I go into these periods or live in different environments, I find myself referring back to the Knowledge Cube and extract parts of the system of the reading habits—any particular aspect of what the Knowledge Cube made me feel or the drive I obtained from the whole concept and principle behind it.

THE BIRTH OF THE KNOWLEDGE CUBE

The Knowledge Cube, interestingly enough, came from me being asked to give a talk or session on how to build confidence. I worked in health and social care at the time and had a group of people, including staff and clients, whom I had never done a presentation as such for. However, the organization themselves had a model which they used. When I looked at the materials, I shook my head and I said, "I think that with my own knowledge, my own training and education, and my own know-how, I can give a decent enough presentation, thanks." And I smiled.

I took note of the information, however, and while keeping it in mind, I decided to prepare the presentation my way. I showed up and did a PowerPoint presentation. I took the materials there and presented in front of my then line manager. Another presentation had been scheduled after mine, but the statement made was: "Can you actually follow that?" And again, I smiled.

I believe I impacted on both the clients and especially the staff at that time. After this session, I discussed this with some of the staff members and they were so impressed that they wanted to share their own ideas. I took that as not merely a compliment but more as an inspirational drive to propel me forward and to carry on my success in presenting and sharing my own knowledge, my own aspirations, and how to make changes in people's lives.

After this session, a decision was made to continue having scheduled presentations. I asked to take the lead and through reading books like *Think and Grow Rich* and other materials from the Napoleon Hill Foundation and Napoleon Hill himself, I toyed with the idea of knowledge since it popped up many times as the right type of knowledge we need to have. Hence, the knowledge aspect of the Knowledge Cube was born.

It had become quite commonly accepted that thinking outside the box automatically meant you thought differently. I was not very comfortable with that idea. I felt that even if you think differently, it does not necessarily put you in a different place in your life. It is a starting point, perhaps, but I struggle with the view of dissecting, extracting, and actually identifying a difference. Of course, somewhere along the line, the structure and shape of a cube came to mind and I read a little about a cube and how best to dissect one. Again, I tried to connect the points of 'the knowledge' aspects and how to view 'knowledge.'

After that, *The Law of Success* became a huge part of my moulding. And agreeing to myself I said, "Hey, this is what the name's going to be. This is what you are going to be called: the Knowledge Cube." I shared this with other clients whom I worked with at the time and they seemed accepting, although there was some debate and other discussion around it. We tried it thereafter until it became an acceptable principle.

THE CUBE VS THE BOX

Very often, I have had challenges where the people I have worked with or the organisations I have shared my principles and ideas with tried to downplay the whole concept of a cube and thinking outside the cube. At times, you would hear them refer to things like, "Why not simply thinking outside the box?"

I have nothing against thinking outside the box but it's not what I am trying to represent. It's not what I'm trying to share or what I am concerned with. As you read this book, you'll continue to establish a sense of purpose that is personalised to you that I like to think of as individuality. As you think of a cube, consider all the different dimensions. Perhaps even consider where you are right now as you read this book.

Think of your environment. Imagine that you actually sit inside a cube which has many different dimensions. You can move from one dimension to the next. You, as an individual, are able to think differently and still seem a human being and an individual. It's not 'crazy thinking' at all. Instead, it's 'extraordinary.' You are not a distraction but someone who collaborates and works as a team. You gain these accolades and praises from others because your thought process is different. You don't try to pretend that you're better than anyone. You are actually in a different place, a better state, a different mind-set. Perhaps you already know, like a personal path that you want to pursue.

Compare this to thinking outside a box . . . a box or a square. Of course, if you want to remove yourself from a square area, maybe this room, or this spot where you are right now, you can move physically, but what does it do for you? Does it make you feel different? Does it put you in a better state of mind? Does it create a better mindset for you? Merely shifting physically or trying to think differently or simply moving your thoughts to something else do not necessarily recreate you.

A box is a box. It is an enclosed area. You can only shuffle within it. Whereas with the concept of the cube—the

Knowledge Cube—you live in different dimensions, whether you move physically or mentally, and you exceed in a way that you shine and that you progress exponentially.

THE KNOWLEDGE CUBE SUCCESSES

I would say that I am one of the very early successes of the Knowledge Cube. However, I cannot take credit for it all. There were clients I worked with in health and social care and other people who were homeless and took the time to come to my sessions. I created a platform to share their own experiences as I guided them and coached them into reading and igniting their own interests. This was a process of recreating that spirit of wanting, of achieving, and of succeeding again in life. And throughout this, I have worked with them and looked on. I have seen some young people, and the elderly as well, being able to make a huge difference and transformational changes in their own lives.

Continuing to work with clients in my work environment, I was able to guide them and direct them on their path to success. As simple as moving from the stage of homelessness back into society, whether it was the outcome they were looking for or not, they were able to leave with my impact in their lives, with them feeling and being and developing into a new person.

Particularly, I could mention the fact that I have had people who pursued studies in education, teaching professions, legal and law studies, becoming coach and bus drivers, getting through probationary periods, and getting past some difficult times. Other people whom I have worked with have had the unfortunate experience of arriving in the

UK as refugees and having to start their lives all over again. They have all made huge strides and transformed into new individuals.

One particular client I have met, Sun *(name changed)*, was originally from the eastern provinces. After leaving the establishment, we have kept in contact. He did share a lot from his own experience as well. He has been in businesses for himself; he has travelled around the world on tours in circus and acrobatic settings. He helped me to 'open my eyes' and see the world and people's lives in a different way in a different world, a different environment, that I did not really know existed. Even though, in terms of mass area, he came from a huge country that I had only read about in ancient books

I have been able to meet some famous people through him. When you look at Sun's journey and his particular successes, several years older than me, he considered me his young friend as I had helped him regain and restart his life.

An experience such as this actually changed me within myself and gave me a successful feeling and as if I had already achieved my purpose with the Knowledge Cube.

THE POWER OF KNOWLEDGE

Growing up, I once heard a song called "The Power of Love." Particularly, the whole idea of power comes to mind. What you know is what you know. Yet you believe that you know more than you think you know. Wherever you are right now, look around and simply focus for a minute on the fabric, the structure, and the environment.

Perhaps you have never actually taken time out to give it much thought. Perhaps you never focused on that particular thing. However, where did this knowledge come from? Did you simply find it? Was it not there within you all the time?

And as I proceed to help you establish how power is within you—how, by you extracting a series of information or complexities of information—you can actually create knowledge by putting this array of information together and putting it into action or a flow.

Knowledge becomes power when you act on that information and knowledge. This happens when you establish that, "Hey, this really makes sense. Hey, I can do this." Or the fact that, "Hey, I am doing something quite different here, right now!"

THINKING OUTSIDE THE CUBE

As indicated earlier, the Knowledge Cube is based on this huge principle of thinking outside the cube. As previously touched on, the world is made up of a vast array of environments and thought processes or different dimensions of thinking. Sometimes, we call it cultures, or we call it way of life, and at times, we refer to it as having habits.

When the Knowledge Cube was created and the whole concept of thinking outside the cube came about, the idea was for people to regain their individuality but with a sense of support where they could have a buddy system or a support network, a support environment to help them progress. To help them feel like, "Hey, I'm different, but I'm still part of it." Or, "Hey, I'm different, but I'm still one of."

Or, “Hey, I’m different, but you are too, and we are in this together.”

So thinking outside the cube doesn’t make you think or position yourself outside the norms of life. It makes you choose a different path, maintain that path, be supported on that path by your network, and grow as the person you want to be. Thinking outside the cube also involves a purposefulness where you can actually retrain and regain a brand-new thought process, a brand-new path to success, and the unique person whom you are happy with.

When I first thought of thinking outside the cube, it did initially sound a little crazy. At least, according to some the critics. Additionally, it did sound a little out of this world. These are some types of reactions you will get when you make a difference. When you actually make a huge difference in society, in different cultures, and particularly in your life, you will not always do what everyone expects you to do. You will not behave as everyone expects you to. However, you will stand out amongst others and you will maintain a different mindset altogether.

Please take some time to reflect and consider how your own thought process differs from some of the peers around you or other co-workers or friends who have an influence on your life.

WHAT IS THE KNOWLEDGE CUBE?

The Knowledge Cube is based on this principle and concept of thinking outside the norm or thinking outside what is expected. I will give you an example: Throughout our lives, there is a system that was created a long time ago that as a young child, you go to kindergarten or you go into child care and you move up the ranks through the education process. These include from childcare, to the nursery school system, through primary school, perhaps secondary school or some sort of tertiary education, and further into college and university level education.

I know there are some people who have gone through that process and perhaps we can call them successful. They have succeeded in their own right, in their own experience, and in their own minds, according to society. They have succeeded according to the acceptable norm and the acceptable system of education within their environment.

The Knowledge Cube, on the other hand, tends to look at people, including children, as the population at large. It tends to look at the whole education system where this process as mentioned does not particularly exist in real life. Most of us are aware—as you are yourself at this stage, and you reading this book tells you as well—that this system is not fool proof or that it is no successful norm as is expected. There is no smooth process from nursery through to primary, secondary, and tertiary education such as college or university.

The Knowledge Cube is created to help people feel confident and accept that they still have a purpose. They still have a place, whether in society, in their lives, or on their success path, to achieve even if they think outside the norm. It connects as well to the view of the mastermind.

The Knowledge Cube, in simple black and white, is a group of people—because you need at least two—coming together. Hence, they may buddy-up or pair-up with a common view of making a difference. Therefore, they work together and they think outside the norm, coming together and thinking outside the cube.

If you look at a cube and the shape of a cube in particular, you see that—and I will show you at different stages—you can extract a square shape or, in particular, a triangle out of a cube. In fact, the cube is made of many triangles and several squares.

REFLECTIVE NOTES

Identify one message I received from this chapter:

How does this make me feel?

Who will I speak with to assist me?

What actions can I take right now?

Go to – **www.TheKnowledgeCube.info**—*to discover more*

CHAPTER 4
THE IMPACT OF READING

DO I REALLY NEED TO READ?

We all need to read. I need to read. You need to read. Whether or not you want to is another question for you to answer. I need to read to keep developing and growing. As a leader, I have been warned in the past that, "if you do not read, you cannot share anything productive." In fact, if you have not read a book in the last week or two, what new information would you have to share with anyone? If you say you want to be successful, why do you think you don't need to read?

While I grew up, I spent a good portion of my time hating to read. One reason for this was the fact that I had bad eyes. I needed glasses (and you can laugh). As such, it hindered me from enjoying reading and experiencing a wealth of knowledge. It prevented me from gaining new experiences and especially those of others before me and of those who have succeeded. I know now that I need to read in order to continue to develop within my area. In order to have more impact or to be more beneficial and of higher value to you or anyone in particular, I must read.

What about you? Why do you think you need to read? Have you given this any thought recently? In fact, do you think you can be successful without reading? If so, how? Reading is important. Reading is necessary. Perhaps you can see it or maybe not. Ask anyone who is guiding you. Ask someone whom you want to emulate. Ask anyone who has been successful or has accomplished anything, especially within your selective areas. Then answer this question: “Do I really need to read?”

Perhaps you may be driving and if you are not at this stage, observe a driver. When you do, realise there are signs and indicators. This is one definite area in which you can see the need to learn to read or to be able to read. As I write this book, at this minute, at this time, I can see signs on buildings and I can see signs on roads. As I look through the window, I see logos, advertising, and directions. And something that we often need is directions.

Why not ask yourself, “What if I cannot read?” And answer the question, “Do I really need to read?” How would you find your road to success if you really don’t need to read?

MENTORS’ ADVICE ON READING

Having a mentor is like a gift. They are not cheap, but when you have them, if they are free or volunteer their time, use them to the best of your ability. I have had my share of unpaid mentorships. I have paid for some of my mentoring in the early stages of my development. I have had guidance and been coached and mentored with no immediate or upfront charge. Either way, I always had to commit. I always had to give an account for what I did. I always had to track my progress.

The impact of reading has guided me toward a mentoring process. Mentors often guide you on the best set of reading materials. They may direct you on what to read and why you should choose that kind of material. Having a mentor, as indicated, is a blessing. However, if you look at it, having a mentor is also like having someone holding your hand, guiding you, and carrying you on your journey. If you choose a mentor wisely, your mentor would have achieved within your scope or your target areas. In fact, mentors are successful because they follow their own practice.

Mentors advise you on how to develop a reading pattern. In the Knowledge Cube, we advise people to start with five to ten pages per day to begin with or fifteen minutes per day. If you do this continuously, you will definitely improve your reading. Your pattern of reading, your reading guide, and your own personal development will improve.

One particular piece of advice I remember receiving from one of my mentors is that when you choose what you read, ensure that you can feel or place yourself within that setting. For example, if you are reading a story about adventure biking, imagine yourself on that adventure or actually riding a bike or in the process.

Mentors try to keep it real. They try to keep you focused and to keep you in control of what you are doing. They may not physically hold your hand but would like you to know that they are there for you as a go-to person if you are slightly deviating or getting off track. They are there to remind you and direct you or keep you in line with what you set out to do and in achieving your success.

I like to think of it as mentors keeping a light ahead of you, or a fire to help you. Imagine a wood fire that keeps burning to keep you warm.

READING AND SUCCESS

I have read myself to success. I remember the first time I learned to drive while I worked in a mechanic shop. My friends at the time refused to allow me to get into a vehicle without their direction or their help. One day, I got so frustrated, I opened a car manual and decided to read it. I do not know what I expected, but because I was somewhat technical, I found myself reading this manual and understanding how the car worked and all the different sections on how to change the gears.

In all honesty, I am not sure I learned how to drive, but I remember getting into a vehicle at the repair shop at that time and I think I simply placed my right foot on the accelerator and pressed downward. I can remember stopping abruptly, shaking because of the speed. The car moved quickly and where I had stopped was at a dangerous spot. Since then, I have followed through on the correct procedure on learning to drive and getting my licences, and I have been driving since.

I cannot sit here and say that I was successful reading through that guide or manual and learning to drive or earning my driver's licence. However, since reading through that guide, I have been very technical when it comes to driving and about vehicles as a whole. The information that I learned probably over twenty years ago, I still retain. No one taught me that. I read that. Today, because of my technical side, some people think I am more skilful than I actually am.

However, I was weak in some areas of my schooling and especially in some of my subject areas. The best way I found to counteract this or to improve was to read. Of course, I was a little shy and sometimes, I found myself not hearing or, perhaps, not listening to what the teacher was saying. As a result, I will find myself trying to read to catch up. It did not always work, but every time I read, I improved in something else and some other aspect of the knowledge area.

I can truly say that I became more successful because of my reading. Over the years of reading different materials and being guided on what to read, I have grown to develop a wide array of knowledge. I have grown and learnt how to take command in some aspects of my knowledge areas or certain topics. I have built a passion, a drive, and an enthusiasm that has allowed me to influence many people's lives. I have been able to inspire others.

THE KNOWLEDGE CUBE READING GUIDE

The Knowledge Cube, when established, focused a lot on building confidence. Although it was based on the Napoleon Hill Foundation's principles, we focused, with my direction, on a series of books for people at different levels. A book was recommended for ten to sixteen-year-olds (tweens-to-teens). Another book was recommended for young adolescents. In addition, other books were included depending on field or intellect, and we later had others added.

In fact, I remember at one time I had recommend books

by Robert Kiyosaki—*Rich Dad Poor Dad*, or the *Cashflow Quadrant*. Another book was on Richard Branson, *Screw It, Let's Do It.* And I did have *Think and Grow Rich* for the more highly enthusiast. Other books were selected based on your interest areas. The particular book was selected based on a review or assessment of what you were looking to achieve. I guided people in their direction. I would then have and do a short review with you to help you with your accountability.

I created an accountability process to help you to keep on track, keep in line with what you committed to do in the first instance, and to help you with a sort of hidden guide. Instead of physically having someone to hold your hand, you had or were able to maintain an image of why you had to get this done in small chunks. I would instead help to create a system as if to hold your hand, guide you, and direct you on what to do and it was there as a support mechanism.

As indicated earlier, the Knowledge Cube was based on your journey on a different thinking path and different mind-set, if you would allow for some coaching. We guided your reading and reviewing, your sharing, and particularly, your exploring. Your inner experiences, changes as you read, and improvements in your knowledge and your success. Although we did not provide you with coaches or mentors, they were always available upon request or agreement. Alternatively, with the buddy system, you were still able to commit in some ways and have an opportunity to be able to account for your progress.

Why not try making a note of some things that you would like some guidance on at the end of this chapter?

WHAT TO READ

I will say read anything and everything. I was once told that reading is for the brain and our mind what exercise is to the body. And if this is correct, why aren't we reading more if we want to have a healthy brain or healthy mind? I have also heard one of my earlier mentors allude to the fact that, "the person who does not read does not have any advantage over a person who actually is unable to read." For some people, reading is a privilege. For other people, well, reading is a wealth of opportunity that they would love to gain.

You can be guided on what to read through by mentors or coaches. Other people can guide you. Perhaps your parents, a guardian, an instructor, a trainer, or a teacher. However, make certain that whomever is guiding you on what to read actually has an interest in your particular target areas or goals. Ensure that they know what you are interested in and that they are not actually directing you to read what they think is good for you.

We need to read. You need to read. I read. Reading is good because it ensures that the things that you are missing, those gaps, can be filled. Use a student in a classroom as an example. The instructor or trainer is speaking and is directing but you are not very clear on what is happening. By reading that particular book in that subject area, you can fill the gaps and learn a lot more of what's happening. You could learn by reading perhaps more than you are taught, by being lectured to, or by being told to or directed to.

Reading is important so, in choosing what to read, I suggest that you choose something that is healthy. Healthy to the mind and healthy to what you are doing—specifically in that area in which you are looking to exceed. Of course, you can read widely or in a broad perspective, but you want to read what is beneficial to you. How do you know what is beneficial to you? Find something that you are interested in. How does it make you feel?

With the Knowledge Cube concept, we do direct people on how best to find good materials to read. We personalise your reading so you know what you're interested in or what you're trying to prove or achieve. So, when choosing what to read, ensure that it has something to do with your own interest area, your own desires, and your own success.

I read mostly books that help me to develop as an individual and as a professional. I can use the knowledge I gain to share or improve someone's life because it has impacted positively on my life.

WHERE TO FIND THE RIGHT BOOKS

Books are often kept in a library. This no longer needs to be limited to a physical structure or a geographic library location. At present, books are accessible through virtual means or electronic libraries. They are in electronic form, in visual form, and even in audio. You can have companions reading to you, which could be fun. You can even select different voice types to read to you in the form of audio books. This has now become beneficial when you are driving, running, walking, or engaged in any other type of exercise activities. Even when you are travelling, sitting, or trying to relax, you can access books with very limited effort. You can have someone read a book to you in total audio format.

However, this does not mean that you cannot find the

good old black and white literature or hardcover books. These are often bought online now through marketing sites. At the time of writing, a vast array of books is still being downloaded electronically and streaming via the Internet. I often direct people on trying to use an environment that's suitable for reading.

If you want self-help books, they are specifically labelled in that area. If you go to a library or you're sorting through categories, you can find books in those areas. Whether you search for them or you're directed to them, ensure that the way you find your books is legitimate and has great value.

Books are located all around us. Very often, I find myself in different neighbourhoods and in different town centres looking at books. It has gotten to a stage where books are given away for free. I must insist, though, that you ensure that books, in whatever format and whether they are free, cheap, or sold to you in any form or promotions, are beneficial to you. Books gifted to you may be found in workshops, or in numerous leadership programmes. They are now associated with a number of series of activities. Often, I have noticed that the best place to find books is where you are looking. Be proactive, search, and seek what you are actually trying to achieve.

WHY READING IS GOOD

I have been reading, or at least committing to read, for the last several years, although it has not always been consistent. Reading has changed my life. It has taught me to be and to do. Reading has developed me and moulded me into a new being. I did not always like reading. I hear from different people and some who have experienced similar effects, that they believe the fact that "reading is to the brain what exercise is to the body." If you will agree, it seems like we should be reading a lot more if we are to maintain a healthy brain and healthy mind.

You simply would not get some things in life so easily unless you read. When I talk about reading, I am not saying to open a book and start reading if you do not have any interest in it at all. I am actually referencing the idea of reading any particular piece or any particular writing that's within your interest area. It could be a magazine. It can be a brochure. Whatever you choose, make certain that you choose those that are within your interest areas.

I recall the inspirational saying that: "the person who does not read, really has no advantage over the person who cannot read." With that said, I believe there has to be something good in reading. Perhaps reading is a privilege for some, whereas it is wealth to others. Some people cannot read. Many times, I have observed people with newspapers—whether on public transport, under their arms, or poking out of their bags—and I am convinced that some of them simply can't read or at least have difficulties. Others have magazines or some financial-type newspapers and they actually only look at graphs, photos, or headlines for some form of activity.

Reading has surely changed my life. There were times when I hated reading. As I indicated before, I've hated reading for a number of reasons. At one time, I found that every time I opened a book to read, I often find myself wanting to simply close my eyes to sleep. I would then put the book down and I would lose interest. I did try, however, to find other pieces or literature that was within my interest areas and I found those helpful because they actually had photographs, some attractive pictures, or other visuals.

Perhaps when you start reading or immerse yourself in reading materials that are of interest or have an impact on your life, you too can experience why reading is good and why it's necessary that you read. Ask anyone who love reading, or who can see the benefit in reading, and they too may tell you why reading is good.

For yourself—yes you!—start reading again! Start seeing the potential you have when you start reading and developing your own habit of reading.

REFLECTIVE NOTES

Identify one message I received from this chapter:

How does this make me feel?

Who will I speak with to assist me?

What actions can I take right now?

Go to – **www.TheKnowledgeCube.info—***to discover more*

CHAPTER 5

BOOK IMPACT REFLECTIONS

HOW READING IMPACTED ON MY LIFE

I can share with you today that I hated reading. Of course, I've shared before that there appeared to have been some problems with my eyes that I wasn't aware of. I had 'tired' eyes. And even though I still have tired eyes at times, I have maintained the drive I have within myself, the enthusiasm, and the interest levels. These come from me learning and improving and getting excited about reading. I suppose I ought to give credit to my mentorship as well. My reading through direction from mentors and other leaders has helped me to discover value in the right books to read.

In fact, in my travelling, I like to peek around and observe the people at train stations handing free stuff out to commuters and passers-by, particularly the distribution of what seemed like free newspapers and other free literature. I often wonder how many people actually pay attention to what they are reading. And I say this because of my own experiences. In the initial stages, I would take a newspaper, look at the back, check all the sports, maybe a few ads, maybe the headline stories, and that newspaper was of no use to me again.

When I was younger and even now, I like looking at the pictures in magazines and I would not generally read the entire magazine as such. When I do choose to read a book, I will select one that I think will be relevant to me, one I believe will affect my life and that I would be very interested in and indulge in. In fact, my getting back into reading and my getting excited about my interest in reading has made me more aware of some things that I have been missing.

Through reading, I was able to expand my ideas and my thought process. I found the enthusiasm, the interest in wanting to create different programmes, and generally, wanting to help people. I recognize that reading has opened my mind. I had one mentor, David Rutz, who applied an analogy and compared my reading as part of my 'mindware'—similar to that of software for computers.

Having worked with this mentor and leader, David *(Escape of Youngevity)* and having met and worked with his family, I experienced what it was like to open businesses and launch new products. Therefore, I always remember his analogy of the mindware. He would explain how reading and books are like our mindware, and how we, as humans, needed to be upgraded at different times. Just like our computers and our software, we needed to be updated or upgraded.

What I realize too is that we often need more mindware or more information. We must, however, get the right type of information or else we will probably end up with a virus or something damaging—some damaging and destructive information.

And for this reason, I often share that it is very important that I read the right literature and materials that will impact positively on my life.

READING FOR SUCCESS

I believe that you can read your way to success. Furthermore, reading is not only the initial stage. By reading, we tend to trigger an integral of our 'Audio-Visual learning experience.' This takes me back to an old research work by Mr Dale Edgar in the 1960s. Why not have a look at this 'Cone Of Learning.' Parts of reading have to do with you actually experiencing something first-hand. By reading, you will become part of that Passive–Active personal process. You get to generate energy, excitement, and fulfilment from that personal experience.

Reading triggers different action points within yourself. It makes you want to do more and achieve more. When you're reading the right book, it directs you to focus more on your own tasks and your own success. As you reignite that wish or desire for reading and continue your reading process, consider what you choose to read. Select the right books, the right materials, and the right literature. Consider why you are reading what you're reading. And particularly, why not consider this: "How will this book, this information that I'm reading through right now impact on my Life, my Success, and my goals?"

Whether you choose to read a sports book, a novel, a self-help book, a workbook, or any book that involves activities or general experiences, ask yourself how these books will impact your success, your future, your goals, and your activities. Reading for success will encourage you to expand on your ideas and on your goal. In fact, it will get you on a path that is inside your path—a path that gets you back on track toward your goal and toward your success.

Why not consider at the end of this, after reading the points and some of the experiences, what has influenced you and how it will have an impact on your success.

THE BOOK IMPACT EXPERIENCE

Books have impacted lives in many ways. As such, I would like you to consider this the next time you read or the next time you listen to someone else's story about what they have read. Imagine that you have not read for a long time, you pick up that one book, and whatever you read in that book makes such a huge impact in your life as well that it turns your entire life around.

What if you didn't pick out that one book? What if someone didn't share that story from that one book that they read? Remember that books—and literature, as such—can often make a huge impact on our life. We never know when that inconsequential or little phrase, or words, or sentence can have a lasting effect. It could be what we're looking to hear or need to hear that day, in that moment, and that it makes us think and act.

I can remember from my experiences in sharing my ideas while working with young people and adults and in different sessions how they've contemplated suicide. How they've contemplated leaving their partners and relationship. How they've contemplated leaving school, leaving a classroom, leaving a job. And how simply, by someone else sharing from their experience of what they'd read, or what they'd done, they were able to use what they'd heard and how it made a huge turnaround in their lives.

I have read a number of books, including self-help books that my mentors directed me to read. In addition, I have overheard other people's conversations of what their experience were like after reading. And as I've picked up some of these books and read through them, I cannot say I loved all of them. However, I've read through them and connected. Even if it was only a paragraph, a few sentences, or a chapter, it may not make a difference if you are affected. Today, I know that it does not matter what you read, at times, as a book will impact on your life whether it be negative or positive. Whether or not it makes a huge difference in your life, I know it can definitely bring about a massive change.

So the next time you pick up a book, choose what you're reading. Consider and select the next book you're going to read to help with that influence you will experience. When you've indulged in your reading, why not recite few sentences? Stop for a moment and breathe as you read. You could be doing that right at this moment. Yes, that which I have just said—what you have just read, what you just imagined, what you're thinking about right now. That particular phrase, thought, or sentence. How is it affecting your thought process, your life, and you in general? How is it impacting on you? Consider this and at the end of this, think, "How has this book impacted on me today?"

THE REAL IMPACT OF READING

I thought it necessary to share that I have identified that there is actually a difference in my experience of the real impact of reading and the 'Book Impact experience.' The real impact of reading indicates real stories that you, me, or anyone for that matter, have experienced. One particular impact I've found with reading is that it increases your knowledge base, of course. Eventually, it enhances your ability to have better conversations. It makes you aware of things that are not exactly in front of you right now so it expands your knowledge. Ultimately, it educates you.

Your reading this book will educate you in several ways and on a number of things. They might be simple things. It might draw your attention to a vast variety of experiences, other people's stories, and my story. It will definitely impact you and your story. Reading at this moment in time is having an impact on you right now. Is your experience right now not real? What are you feeling right now? What you're reading right now and what you're thinking about right now is relative. So what do you want to do right now? Whatever you want to or are going to do after reading is the real impact of your reading today.

The next time you pick up a magazine, a newspaper, or another book, read at least a paragraph. Whatever it is you choose to read, a story for instance, as you follow on, imagine how you feel after you've read that paragraph or perhaps this paragraph. Grasp how it can change your life or how it can recreate feelings that you may have suppressed. How it recreates or connects with your own senses. Why not consider too how much of a difference it's brought you and your mindset now that you've read it.

One story I particularly remember from reading comes from a leadership exercise I've been involved in. One person shared their experience of standing next to one of the past presidents of the United States of America as he shared a book title that he had read and how that one story changed his life. But who initially read the story? And who mentioned the story? Why is it even influencing your life right now? Why does it make you think? Why are you considering or reconsidering different things and different decisions?

Whatever you read and whatever you experience when you read, there is no doubt that it creates or stirs something that is real.

THE KNOWLEDGE CUBE BOOK IMPACT

I have read several books that actually made a huge impact on my life. When I finally decided on the Knowledge Cube concept, I was exposed to the work of the Napoleon Hill Foundation. I uncovered the principles in books such as, *Think and Grow Rich* (Hill), *How to Win Friends and Influence People* (Dale Carnegie), and other books by Robert Kiyosaki. It was as if I had a complete shift in my knowledge and awareness. I adopted these authors and books within the programme and within our sessions. I generally encouraged everyone to read widely and to purposely select literature by successful people such as Sir Richard Branson, Napoleon Hill, Dale Carnegie, and Robert Kiyosaki, to name a few.

These successful people, and particularly their books, have shifted my self-esteem, my awareness, and my self-worth. They influenced how I think about myself, how I carry myself, and how I believe within myself that I can achieve. And as the Knowledge Cube Book Impact progressed, we (the team) were able to make clients more focused on why they should read. This allowed them to learn from other people's experiences and the impact their reading had on them.

They discovered how simple, small information, small and what seemed like insignificant events, could actually have such impact on someone else's life when they read. When they engross themselves in a decent book or whenever they learn to study a book or writing materials or literature, especially within their interest areas, these impact their lives.

I will share this story with you about one young man I once met. He said, "Andrew, you're truly my friend. Since I have been coming to your Knowledge Cube sessions, it's been making me think about what I really want to do. Of course, I want to get my degree in education, but I'm starting to think I want to be a teacher." And while I smiled, he said, "Andrew, can you mentor me?"

Of course, I felt elated at the fact that this young man would want to choose me at that time to mentor him. And the fact that he saw that kind of quality in me. However, while I was on my journey, I asked him to focus on getting his degree, finishing what he was doing, and if he had the time, to continue supporting me with the Knowledge Cube, and I would continue to give him some guidance and directions. I did not want to be referred to or be known as his mentor just yet.

He later shared that he found it difficult in the general libraries to locate some of the books I suggested he read. He further indicated his gratitude and went on to share how he was pleased with me for helping him become more aware and helping him to seek other knowledge apart from what they taught him in the classroom. And specifically, he stated that, "Because of you, Andrew, I feel like I want to read more and share more."

THE KNOWLEDGE CUBE BOOK REVIEW

I created the Knowledge Cube Book Review sessions some years past. It was while leading some life-skills training with a client group. One of the first sessions I ever held was actually with people who faced homelessness. They were being temporarily housed within shelters and hostels, or life houses, as the name changes. It was meant to be simple sessions. I brought some folks of different cultural backgrounds together in one a room, and I look back and think of it as a phenomenal experience and activity. They all shared generally from their reading experiences.

These sessions included reading books selected by the Knowledge Cube team and me, so everyone was able to share from similar books. I can say that each person's experience and sharing revealed that everyone who reads the same book experiences something different. Everyone who reads a book will give different views or reviews on that book because it speaks to them differently.

It is necessary that I indicate that today, the Knowledge Cube is constantly evolving. I will continue to direct you on specific areas to focus on and to consider when you reflect on your journey. I would encourage you to not so much review the book or review what is in the book that you have read, but rather to identify and connect with the changes it brings to you in your life. Of course, you might deviate and want to look at the texture, the feel of the book, the make-up of the book, and the colours. All these, if you really want to go into it, do connect with some feelings you have as your senses become heightened.

Sometimes, you ignore the simple things that touch our lives. This book you are reading right now, the materials involved, the pages and voice you hear, all come from somewhere and are in fact, significant to your experience. They derive from natural elements so nature is initially intended. The colours connect with something that you can think of or something that you can see and smell. That scent—and I'm not suggesting that you go and literally smell the book pages—that you smell right now is all part of your experience of reading this book. It is not coincidental.

As you review or simply think of what you just read or what you're reading right now, consider how the words can create a passion within you or arouse your feelings. Why not ignite this feeling? Give it a spark to want to take action. A yearning of wanting to do something towards your goal. Chase after what you want to achieve in life right now.

The Knowledge Cube Book Review encourages you to connect with 'your own self.' Your personal self-esteem, your own self-worth, and your own belief system need to align. Your own success, dreams, and goals need to face in one direction. Why not take a few minutes to reflect on this direction after you've read this chapter?

WHY PEOPLE DON'T READ

We often don't read because we lack interest, we lack wisdom, or we lack direction. I have found that we tend not to read because we don't know how to read. Of course, there are some people who, I have to accept, cannot read for particular reasons. There are still some people who never learned to read and that could change by learning how. Yet there are others who choose not to read. This can simply be from stubbornness, from busyness, from lack of interest, or any other reasons you can have for not reading.

Often, people don't read because of busyness. They say, "Oh, I'm busy." Or, "I am too busy." Or, "I don't have the time." I classify these as excuses, even if they're genuine excuses.

Some people don't read because they lack direction in what to read. They may pick up the wrong book or the wrong material, start reading it, and lack interest immediately. They may even pick up something exciting and wander off into it. It could be a magazine. It could be graphics, cartoons, or adult- type magazines, but anything that is filled with stories and photographs and excitement about other people's lives. I refer to them as gossip magazines or gossip literature.

People don't read because they're so engulfed in these materials very much linked to television or particular real-life shows, or even the everyday buzz. One very interesting reality I've come to be aware of is that some people don't read because they lack interest. Lacking interest is one of the biggest excuse, or worst excuses, I could imagine for why people do not read. It is such a lame excuse that it's practically a lie.

Imagine how much we lie to ourselves about not reading. Perhaps one of them is the simple fact that we may not pay attention to what we are doing or saying. You are literally reading here right now, are you not? So if you say you do not read, in a sense you are not conscious of what you are saying. The main fact is that you may simply lack interest and don't pay attention. You are lacking in what is very necessary—reading.

REFLECTIVE NOTES

Identify one message I received from this chapter:

How does this make me feel?

Who will I speak with to assist me?

What actions can I take right now?

Go to – **www.TheKnowledgeCube.info**—*to discover more*

CHAPTER 6
POETRY 'N RHYTHM

CAN YOU WRITE A POEM?

I can recall how intrigued I was with poetry and poem writing from the early days of attending school. At times, I laughed because I did not really understand the works of, say, Shakespeare in my early childhood. As I got through to secondary school and into college, I learned the importance of poetry and poems.

I remember sitting down with my English professor after taking an English class in college. She had asked me, "Andrew, why did you write with all those words?" Note here that at times, I felt that if I wrote with all those complicated words that I would sound important. As if I would sound like I belonged to a higher authority or like I belonged to a higher knowledge group. Like an important aristocrat, I must say.

The thought now makes me chuckle. And I remember when she insisted: "Andrew, sit here and write a poem, please. Use the simplest language. Think of when you were not a college student." This, then, was not a case where I was able to simply laugh anymore or play the fool.

So I started to write as I thought and the poem was about 'bussing it,' as in catching the bus. I was being jokingly expressive at the time. But it put me in a happy place. And so, I commenced writing and it was like, 'I got up in the morning, getting ready to go to school and bussing it. I'm going to grow up and go to work, without my car and I'm bussing it. I sit, I watch everyone commuting and many bussing it. And as I look at my neighbours running to get to work, they're bussing it.' And I closed the poem off and I show it to my professor.

She asked me, "Andrew, can you see the difference with this poem and how naturally it came to you?" I was smiling as she'd taught me to express myself more freely. She said, "Andrew, this is how you are. This is how I want you to be. Have you realised when you're saying your poem, or talking about where you grow up, and in your environment, how happy you were and how free-spirited were you?" I sat there for a little while, smiling, and said, "Yeah." And that 'yeah' came out very slowly, "Ye-a-a-ah," as I thought, 'What's the big deal?'

She further added, "That's how I want you to write." As I was not on the English major course of study, I did not continue her classes later on. My English professor was willing to coach me, and I later reciprocated by agreeing to assist her with some work. While this was at college where professors do not have time for 'non-students' on a limited budget, I remember being selected. I think, while looking back and not necessarily regretting it, I did ask myself, why didn't I simply continue writing?

I can sit here and look at the sky and think of the words, but I'm not into poems. I've seen some incredible work and learnt some of the art of poems from others' experiences. I know, as a young man growing up, when someone mentioned poems or poetry, the first person who probably came to mind was Shakespeare. It took me a while to realise that with any mention of Shakespeare there was poetry, theatre, art, and entertainment.

I realise, as I look into more and more materials, how poems could be such a simple thing. Even now, I think of some rhythms and the words in my head. For example: 'you look up at the sky, it's blue. My feeling right now is blue. I feel every colour may be blue since I also drive a car that's blue.'

I do know that poems have different forms and, of course, with the right coach and the right mentor pointing you in the right direction, you too can learn to express yourself in many ways. Writing, expressing, relieving through dreaming is a beautiful way of writing, and poetry as well. It puts you in a different place and with the Knowledge Cube, you may experience and learn how poem-writing is a silent way of you talking to yourself and being able to hear your own self speak. And, really, without interrupting anyone else. Writing a poem is a means of healing and learning.

And so the question I will ask again is: can you write a poem? Can you? And why not, if you think you cannot. Because if you think you can't right now, you're probably right. And as I've been taught by my mentors, whether you think you can or you can't, you are probably right.

DRUM BEATS

As I think of and share my thoughts of drum-beats, I'm bobbing my head, remembering an old folk rhythm—one I used to hear repeatedly in summer every year in Prospect Park in Brooklyn, New York. During college years, every summer, especially as it's warm and bright, some groups would meet up to beat the drums and dance intermittently in the park. I remember that at times when I passed the park, I would see dust flare up from all the dancing and excitement. And, as I drew closer, I could hear the beating of the drums and the vibes of the rhythm.

Sometimes, it seemed like a spiritual celebratory event, and while they danced it was almost as if they evoked the spirits. The constant beating of the drums reminded me as well of a period growing up, specifically around the Rastafarians. I could reminisce about the old melodies of great reggae music, sounds from Bob Marley and the Wailers, groups like Culture, and bringing it forward to Morgan Heritage.

As I take my thoughts back to the days of my college experiences, I can recall getting into the African-American culture in more depth. My flow of thoughts made me remember the engulfing of the culture and the music and how it speaks about the telling of stories, and of expressing myself. It's about going back to things like poetry and finding your rhythm and making you want to simply get into yourselves. During the instrumental periods on a weekend, that invigorating feeling makes me think too of the integration back into your whole being, your spirit.

Very often, I hear people talk about motivation. From the

Knowledge Cube standpoint, we believe that motivation has to be within and as such, you need to be inspired. Something triggers within you and that's why we like the idea of igniting. That, in itself, sparks that interest back into you.

And so with drum beats, whether you're tapping your feet on a wooden floor or you're tapping on the counter. It could be on the table, the kitchen cupboards, or if you're in the living room or at a desk, or wherever you're sitting right now, simply tap on something and make that beat. And as it becomes a little bit more of a base rhythm, hear your beats.

As I can imagine you trying this I know it will make you move. It will make you want to get out of that slump and that feeling you had before you started reading this. Perhaps you're bobbing your head again and moving different parts of your body, looking for a little rhythm within the drums.

Why not think of what kept you from moving like this or feeling like this? Sometimes, it's merely a little drum beat that is needed. And as the beat gets louder, perhaps you could get back into the music you used to love or the things you liked to do. Maybe it's the books you used to read. Why not get back to dreaming again, wanting again, and recreating that inspiration within you?

As one of my mentors reiterates to me, and I particularly hear the well-renowned Les Brown repeats, "You were born to greatness." Let the drum beat bring you back to your greatness. Let the drum beat give you that rhythm. Let your drum beat inspire you and ignite that flame in you again. And let's get this done.

FINDING YOUR RHYTHM

I smile and I wiggle my toes as I think of this next section because, as I think of finding my rhythm, of course I think of dancing. I think of my own cultural music. I think of music that you hear in your head at times when you're simply in that mood. It could be a tranquil mood. It could be a lazy mood. It could merely be in a nice, relaxed mood.

Sometimes, I like to think of it as or liken it to the idea of my early days and the Shaolin kung fu films. I remember the advancement, heightened interest, and 'hoorah' of exercise like yoga and pilates. I often reflect as if I am reminiscing and see and imagine that smooth, flowing movement. It's almost like a ballet-type flavoured action. That extended, happy but calm, peaceful, and altogether therapeutic kind of movement.

I remember not so long ago, I attempted to learn to dance the lovely Salsa. In fact, it was a mix between Spanish or Latino style dancing of the rumba, which really didn't go down too well. I still like the movement, though. I still like to see the flow and the rhythm. I liken it to a mechanical way that an individual is able to move their limbs and their bodies, and create something very beautiful.

Imagine, as well, listening to some drumbeats—simple little drum beats and any type of instrument but with no words, only the sounds of the instruments playing. And imagine those beats as they play and you listen. Can you connect or identify with them? I am certain that, whether it's a musical instrument or any continuous melody, it will make you want to move some part of your limbs. Perhaps your toes, tapping your feet, or shaking your head or shoulders.

And perhaps, as you get into it, you might want to move other parts of your body as well.

I know, when I listen to music that I like, I'd shake to it or bob my head and eventually, get all the body parts into play. I mean, if you really want to find your rhythm, wouldn't you choose to perhaps listen to something that's of interest to you? For this reason, I will say that in finding your rhythm, you have to get in tune. You have to tap into your own feelings, your own beats, your own melody, your own movements, and your own rhythm.

MICROPHONE CHECK

Microphone check, one, two, one, two. Microphone check, one, two. This is the way I remember it done by artistes, including some rappers, MCs, and speakers who entered a stage to perform. I call it the historical way of checking a mic, the sound, and igniting confidence. It goes back to the nineties, by my recollection, though some individuals say the eighties and the late eighties especially. Either way, going back to as far as the nineties, microphone check, one, two 'revved up' energy. Imagine you're in a club or you're at a social event and they tested the mic and said, "Microphone check," and your favourite artiste or performer entered the stage. Can you envision the energies and the noise?

As you get into it, you realise that rappers and hip-hop artistes automatically create the flow of energies around you. And if you go back to the likes of Dr. Dre and the early days of Eminem, I can reflect on their collaboration. Their timeline together magnifies periods of lasting energies and great influences. The particular reason for referring to Dr. Dre is that as a true entrepreneur, his rising turnarounds of music started with rhythm. In fact, the Knowledge Cube's poetry n' rhythm ideas today started when as I reflected and looked back at the nineties. Imagine, too, the good old microphone check that brought you through to the days of the lovely 'beats' earphones.

I hope you can follow here that very often, it starts with that little whisper, that little phrase, "Microphone check." That's where loads of rhythm started from. And after the microphone is checked, you're in control and it's time to get your audience to listen to the flow and the poetry 'n rhythm. That should be the number one thing—really listen. After you're done with the microphone check, everything is in order. It's easy to imagine that after you have ignited your idea, your view, or your interest—your microphone check—the person who is now listening from the other end is loving what you are after. He is now listening to the beats. I hope you're following here. From the microphone check to the 'beats' headphones, for example, and similarly, from you igniting your passion to your end results or your success.

From the nineties to now, we still see the 'beats' headphones and the connection with the art of opera and the interest of the technology companies. In order for someone to move from that stage of the nineties through their journeys and into such a phenomenal businessperson and entrepreneur through the realms of music, it's clear that rhythm does work.

I mentioned Dr. Dre and the likes of Eminem earlier and if you have that interest, why not have a look at Eminem's film *8 Mille?* Eminem is still building his history and his music. If you think back to the early days, he came out there as someone who didn't seem to amount to much to many people. But he took that mic, did a microphone check, opened up the airwaves, and created a path for others to listen to and respect what he had to say. They came to respect a new voice, a new culture, a new leader, and an entirely new influence in the music arena. At the same time, he remains someone who's still out there, looks different, behaves different, and sounds different. Check his story, and compare your passion areas.

Is there someone like you? Do you have something that makes you stand out, makes you different, and makes you want to be you and gain that respect that you perhaps earn from your own microphone check?

POETRY AND MUSIC

It took me some time while in college, actually, to learn the different origins of poetry through music and, I will add, through music history. I got more in-depth into the whole music arena, rap in America, and calypso and soca music in the Caribbean. Each territory tried to claim ownership of who started or owned the music genres. I explored a little deeper, going back to the periods of Robert Nester or Bob Marley to Louis Armstrong, Frank Sinatra, the 'steel pan' music in the Caribbean, and drum music, especially of Africa. As I delved into the mix of drums and dance in Africa and African-American communities, I came to learn the whole concept of expressing oneself through music.

If you look at some famous—or perhaps, popular—pop artist music enthusiasts, I will refer to them as entrepreneurs as well. Think of the likes of Kanye West and Jay-Z compared to the periods of rappers such as DMX, Ja Rule, and Tupac. I mention these guys because they were labelled persons according to our society and according to us. They represented something, but most of all, I would say they represent powerful messages and the expression of self and poetry.

What these artistes or change-makers have in common is the fact that they used music to wage a war to express themselves, to demand or claim their territory, and to take ownership. This is essentially the thing that business owners and entrepreneurs go after. They claim ownership, try to be outstanding or stand out, whether in society or in their different territories, and display or express who they are and what they stand for.

In fact, they were purely artistes we can call change-makers, and they continue to have impact. In some ways, they had a system of expression and a period in which they earned their respect. All this was through the expression of poetry and music. If you look at and listen to what they were saying and you think back about poetry, they actually used music and poetry to get their message across.

Hence, after a period of reflection and working different groups, I tried to put these two things together and put my message across together with my systems so I could help others achieve, feel the effects, and enjoy this particular art form. I suppose I could say this is when the Knowledge Cube Poetry 'n Rhythm came to being.

POETRY

Poetry, prose, and writing poems were all a huge part of my studies in English language and in English literature while at school. Very often, when you hear of poems or poetry, you hear people refer to Shakespeare almost immediately. I heard it said once that poetry is entertainment for the elites. Whether you use Google or any other search engine, try searching for poetry as a whole. Look at the history aspect of it or some of the famous names behind it and try to understand exactly what it is about. Poetry seems to have an adequate amount of performance and expression surrounding it.

It was used as a form of communication many years ago, primarily by the elite. It was developed and put in different formats to make it and English more fluent. Poetry seemed to make expressing yourself more elegant. While reading this book, why not take a few seconds and think of any previous poems you may have come across. While doing that, remember that poetry in itself is art.

Within the structure of the Knowledge Cube, I like to think of the idea of creating something—of being creative, being expressive, and being articulate. And so, in bringing poetry into this book, I was passionate about the idea of the history behind expressing oneself in different cultures. Moving with the times and focusing on what is current, what do we see in front of us? When we look at the art industry, the music industry, the performance arena, and especially festivals, we see poetry and art being expressed hand-in-hand.

With the Knowledge Cube, I like to direct your attention to your own expression of yourself. Perhaps I can draw your attention to the sky on a nice, sunny evening. Perhaps

I can attempt this: The sky is blue, not as blue as you. The clouds stand high, high in the sky. Some of them still. Some of them will eventually become numerous and form into a still. Is this not poetry? And if not, then what exactly is it? Is it not expressing of oneself in a more eloquent or directed, purposeful, and lyrical manner? Why not consider this for yourself.

THE KNOWLEDGE CUBE POETRY 'N RHYTHM

As we come to the recognition of the Knowledge Cube Poetry 'n Rhythm phenomena, we believed, at the early stages, in bringing people together for a collaboration of expressions. Poetry and rhythm meant something different for every person. Some people were nervous and others were shy. In identifying this—and perhaps even within yourself—remember that there are some people who will always prefer the intellectual side of things. Yet there are others who would rather have the simple black-and-white method of writing in any form. I call it the old black-and-white because we are talking about people who believe it has to be in that 'ole' written format. As the elderly man in the folk song would say: "If it ain't in black and white, then it ain't official."

There are those people who enjoy listening to music and others who will rather tune into their own beats, their own pattern and style, and their own way of doing things. I call this their own rhythm. I needed to figure out a way that through the Knowledge Cube, I could bring these two, say, dimensional ways of getting a better grasp of who you are. Bring them together to create the Knowledge Cube Poetry 'n Rhythm phenomena where you can use music and sound to express yourself and to put yourself out there. Become recognised, get your message across, and live more freely. Whether it be through music, whether it be through writing, more than anything, express yourself, your own ideas, your own concepts, and your own visions.

If you follow me here, I am insisting that you display you with your own poetry and rhythm style of things and pave your way. If you use your senses and get back into your imagery, your vision, and your view, you will be able to profess it, to express it, and to live it. I wish for you to believe and show that you can do this. The Knowledge Cube Poetry ‘n Rhythm will allow you to awaken that message within you, that message you want to share.

REFLECTIVE NOTES

Identify one message I received from this chapter:

How does this make me feel?

Who will I speak with to assist me?

What actions can I take right now?

Go to – **www.TheKnowledgeCube.info**—*to discover more*

CHAPTER 7

WHAT IS HOLDING YOU BACK?

BAGGAGE CLAIMS

I'd like to take this time out to reflect on my experience travelling—of flying, or even using the coach between counties and boroughs in different countries I've travelled to. Perhaps you can recall your own experience. Have you ever noticed how you have to go through all these procedures? Then, when you think it's finally done and you have the 'Yes! I'm free' feeling and are ready to go, there's another process again and another period you still have to go through. This is time you have to spend now to pick up what belongs to you. It's as if you can't go far if you leave it behind as it's yours to claim and to carry.

I liken this to all our experiences in life. All our journeys have some experiences in which there are some actions we have taken, or should have taken, or may have taken, yet we are still uncertain. We must revisit some of those action points, those ifs and buts. We need to somehow revisit them as if they're brand new. What we're really doing is reappearing so we can claim them as ours. If we don't take them at that point and get rid of them or simply carry them along with us, it creates a spiral effect. It may compound itself into something more serious.

Can you imagine leaving your baggage lying about in a train station? If after fifteen or twenty minutes, no-one's claimed it and you're gone on your journey, everyone in security gets busy trying to find who owns it. There are announcements. There are people reviewing footage on CCTV cameras. There are people asking questions. You will leave this spiral of activities that would have been avoided or dealt with differently if you had simply claimed what was yours.

Take what's yours today. Deal with it. Get it out of the way and let the rest carry on. Let it be freed. Let the processes around you flow consistently. If you do this, your journey forward—your way to success, the path that you are going on—tends to be more direct and more consistent and flows in one direction and at a good pace. Even though you have this baggage you've claimed, when you move forward, that weight you thought was too much to carry, that thing that you think you should leave behind, or that thing that you decide to claim and take ownership of, becomes lighter and lighter. It becomes so subtle that it almost disappears.

Claim your baggage. Deal with your highs and lows. Claim what is yours today.

DO NOT STOP YOU!

Very often, at least in my life, I've noticed that we want to achieve something and there are periods you go through, in addition to the highs and lows. These create an inconsequential emotional roller coaster type experience. In taking time out to only invest time and focus on that one thing, reconsider the initial plan, or try to create an alternative path or goal, I find that I slow down so much that eventually, it's as if I stop focusing on my goal altogether. It feels as if I have started rethinking my ideas, questioning and reconsidering and reasoning whether or not to continue and creating ifs and buts.

I have learnt and understand that this 'ifs and buts' mindset is more like creating baggage. It's like creating unnecessary weight to carry around with you. And very often, you can't constantly carry a sizeable weight on your shoulders or on your back, or even in your head,. Many times, what holds you back are mental and emotional weight. And as the saying goes, it's (the) mind over (the) matter. Simply put, it's mental weight that you create that holds you back and stops you.

I'll warn you to not hold yourself back. Stop preventing yourself from progressing. Note that there will always be obstacles. There will always be potholes and you may require continuous repairs, constant reminding, and periods of difficulties. Some ups and downs will actually help get us through to the end.

I share with you at this stage that wherever you're at in your life and with your goal, do not stop you. Whatever you're trying to achieve, I warn you at this stage, do not stop you. Do not stop you achieving. Do not stop you reaching that goal. Do not stop you making that first step or that next step or that final step that you probably need to reach what I call your 'final destination,' to reach your ultimate goal, your ultimate point you need to get to. To feel and be successful and celebrate, do not stop you!

DON'T HOLD YOURSELF BACK

Very often, you will meet obstacles. Imagine that while driving, you might meet a pothole or even a barrier, let's say due to roadwork. What will you do? Perhaps It may be as simple as passing an exam and you are unable to excel at that. Or even failing a class that you need for the next semester and you feel you can't get by this stage. Every decision you make will allow you to go forward or hold you back. If you quit, it is a decision. If you choose to go forward, it is also a decision. And If you do nothing, that too is a decision that you are making. It's all choices. Only you can make the ultimate choice. I once heard that when you quit a situation, you are actually creating a permanent solution to your problem and you don't actually move forward with that particular project.

We tend to hold ourselves back in different ways. I have worked with people in the past who, because of immigration issues, work permit issues, being unable to work or restricted to work, got so hung up on these types of personal situations. They have stopped them self from progressing one way or the other. It may be that there are restricted hours in which to work and they choose not to work. It may be that they have a restriction on what kind of work they do, but they moan, stress and find excuses for no improvement in themselves instead of choosing to make changes in their life circumstances.

What I've seen in this kind of situation is that only you

can make that ultimate decision. When you choose to do nothing, you hold yourself back. When you choose to create barriers, you hold yourself back. When you choose to quit, you hold yourself back.

I have learnt once that time management is not our problem, but self-management. Since time is constantly changing, we need to move with the times. And time loss can never be regained. When we choose to not progress, we lose time. When we choose to create more obstacles, we lose time. We hold ourselves back in such a way that it becomes habitual. Then we create a circumstance where everything seems not to be in our favour. Everything seems not so good and we find difficulty in progressing since we haven't made those preliminary steps.

In every action, every circumstance, and every instance when we make a decision, we are the ones who are choosing. Therefore, I urge you. Please do not hold yourselves back.

HOW TO STOP HOLDING YOURSELF BACK

I have mentioned before how there are some things you don't have control over. Some of them might make you pause in your moment if you are stuck by them or allow them to take charge of where you are right now. This might simply be the way it is. It might cause you to spend not enough time thinking about your goals or even thinking about unnecessary things. It's not that you try to forget it. It might be important matters or serious issues that are going on in your life right now. Either way, there may be things that can definitely hinder you.

If there are some things going on right now and you have

very little control over them, why should you dwell on it? Why should you allow it to stop you? Is there some way that you can go around it and allow it to work its process? At times, you must allow time to do its work and carry on as normal. Why not allow 'it' to happen while you continue on your journey? Very often, you can get so caught up with what's going on around you. Whether or not you do something, the 'it' is still going to happen.

You can simply take a step out of it—and you can literally stand right now and take a step left. Take another step right and consider for a moment that every step you make will move you away from something. It could be a location or the position you are in. If you shift left or right, turn right or left and walk away, it will take you somewhere. What if you take one step forward? And another step? And another step in the same direction? Perhaps you might meet or have some good luck. Yes, you might even meet a pothole or obstacle, which you can probably step over or walk away from. Every step forward you take means you don't remain stagnant and you continue to progress.

As such, I will insist that you focus at all times with the end result in mind. Create that image of what it is that you're trying to achieve right now. What is it that you're working towards? Your goals, your aspirations. Focus on that end result and take little, tiny steps but significant steps toward achieving your goal, meeting your target, and achieving your perfection. Take a step forward and I assure you that this will stop you from holding yourself back.

MY LIFE OF FREEDOM

I can picture my early days, visiting my grandmother on a little island called Canouan. As I reflect and look back on my environment, I envision a white sand beach, clear blue skies, and immaculate white clouds. Altogether, it's beautiful with the bright skies and the glitter of the sun on the sea. I can imagine me, my friends, and other siblings on the beach enjoying a swim and occasionally running about. As I look around, some adults are jogging along the beach and others are exercising on the sand. As I reflect, I can even remember seeing the imprints of their footprints left behind. The calm water comes in, washes it all away, and brings it back to a clear and level surface.

As I reminisce on my younger years, I can recall playing on the beach. It was so much fun taking dives after climbing on the ferries. The picnics and enjoying the view of the ocean. The singing of birds. The occasional times pointing at the dolphins as we journeyed between islands on excursions. I can remember as a child how I was being picked up and taken home, and again, getting home and being able to look over the mountainous regions. All the vegetation, the beautiful views, and most recently, I remember getting into photography as a hobby. This reminded me of when I would go to the heights and take photographs and enjoy the beauty and the feeling of being free.

My Life of Freedom encompasses my life from the Caribbean. I have journeyed to several islands and travelled into North America and parts of Europe. Also, I've been in New York City and Manhattan, along the rivers and going to the parks. The many journeys I've had out of New York, visiting other States. The excited times in Atlanta, Detroit, Connecticut, and I must mention my lovely trip to Las Vegas where I will forever remember the nightlife there. I can recall how beautiful it was and how different it was. Then, I include the varied trips to the Florida state and cruising via Miami and the Bahamas. Finally, being in the UK, travelling from coast to coast and to France, Denmark, and Spain. There is much to be appreciated and call, 'my Life of Freedom.'

I share this with you not to brag or boast about my journeys but to share with you. Anywhere you go is your own life experience, the opportunities that you have had, and you have taken. I am certain that there is much to appreciate in your life. Once you can recall these experiences and adventures, that is your story. It is part of your journey in 'your life of freedom.' If you can picture it, if you can imagine it, if you can create an image around it, then it is your story. Why not take time out today to simply reflect?

I am not putting any timeframe on this. You should take as much time as you need. In fact, why not simply put the book down or consider a pause. Reflect for a few minutes. The beautiful places you have been. The lovely experiences you have had. Different things that have happened in your life and the things that only you can smile or laugh about. As it has been my life of freedom that I have shared with you, how about you? Why not recreate your life of freedom here and now.

STRESS LEVELS

Have you ever tried to measure your stress levels? What about actually moving your stress levels? Yes, to create and manipulate your stress level. Did you know that you could actually control it? You can, whether it goes up or whether it goes down. And you can control it in such a way that if it's too high for you today, you can decide if you want to make it worse or if you want to make it much less.

I am not being ridiculous in any way here. How about we examine who controls your stress levels. There are outside factors. There are internal factors. And very often, I've found that the factors that you can be in control of are what increases or decreases your stress levels. Imagine, for a moment, the outward factors. Things that come from other people. The stuff people try to bring to you.

People's stuff, as I often call it, tends to be those factors that we will take on quite naturally. When we take stuff on board from other people, our stress levels will fluctuate and will go up or go down. It's as if there is a gauge or an on and off switch that literally makes us feel more stressed or in a happier mood.

I suggest that you look at your stress levels by considering your own factors. Take the time out to check within yourself. Why not ask yourself relevant questions? What is there that I need to deal with? What is there in my life that I need to take control of or take action on? What can I remove from my life? What can make my own burden, my mental or psychological burden, much less?

Of course, people will always talk. And if you think people are talking about you, does it really matter? They will talk anyway. People will always worry and people will always cheer you or ridicule you. It's how the world works. And people will always judge you. It is as if you are being sentenced by other people's stress. Those are outside or outward factors, which we have very little control over, and we can simply ignore them.

So I urge you, as you read this chapter, do not allow your own stress levels to hold you back or to hinder your successes. Do not allow your own stress to hinder you recreating that spark. Do not let it stop your smile, that happy face, that happy feeling, or that happy moment. Take your stress level lever all the way down. Let's do this today!

THE POWER OF FEELING FREE

The one thing that has stood out for me and that I continually focused on throughout my leadership training, personal development, and continuous learning, is freedom. I have explored this in a number of ways. Yes, I have enjoyed the experienced of what it is like to fly first class, to drive expensive cars, or to travel, and to meet popular and what we may consider highly important people. What has been more rewarding, specifically, is an awareness when meeting other successful people. Those who excel through their own development and their own successes and have created wealth and impacted on many other people's lives reveal another level of freedom.

While working with one of my mentors, he reiterated to always consider the legacy I want to leave behind. In me seeking success, I've taken the time out to enjoy nature. This may have been a simple walk in the park, visiting or exploring artefacts museums, the zoo, and even art galleries. I have been learning and practising appreciation for the legacy of others.

When you surround yourself with artefacts and history,

it gives you a sense of being and at times, a sense of feeling. Some things you may not be able to experience hands-on but you can have that moment of being in a place where you can feel the surroundings of what it could have been or what is possible. In fact, it is all in having a glimpse of what our ancestors or those before us have created. A real sense of the path they paved for us.

The next time you are driving or riding, whether it is on a ferry, in a car or bus, or even a train, try to experience what it's like with a window view. Have a window down or your face exposed to the wind blowing toward you. It is even better when your eyes are closed, and please, only if it is safe to do so. Perhaps you can close your eyes and even better, if you can do this outside in open space. What about where you are right now? Why not close your eyes and experience this feeling of what it's like to have the wind blow towards you. Smell the air and experience what it's like to be and feel free with nature.

I've experienced this myself while cycling, and at times, while running in the park. I set myself target spots. As I achieve them, I am so elated. It's that feeling. That little feeling that you've achieved something. When you get to your target, that little moment empowers you. It gives you that "Yes!" or awed feeling. It gives you that sense of *the power of feeling free.*

REFLECTIVE NOTES

Identify one message I received from this chapter:

How does this make me feel?

Who will I speak with to assist me?

What actions can I take right now?

Go to – **www.TheKnowledgeCube.info**—*to discover more*

CHAPTER 8

YOU KNOW MORE THAN YOU THINK YOU KNOW

DO YOU THINK YOU CAN KNOW MORE?

Our brain capacity is excellent in many ways. We cannot really use up all the space or all the packets of storage. We can constantly pump information in. A lot of this information has to be processed and goes back out in some way or form. This is why we sometimes listen, gather information, then process it. And we are able to share, to speak, to sing, or write. To express ourselves, our brain is filled with all these packets of information—all the 'stuff' that we put in there, through media and especially from our surroundings. In everything that we do, we are gathering packets of information.

We then can process this information. This is why some of the early thinkers state that thinking is hard work. Very often, we're not thinking about what we're doing or saying. It is such an automated process that we can simply open our mouths and speak. It is in processing the information that we want to share, and processing what we're talking about, that we tend to make sense. We can then acknowledge that we actually experience what we are talking about.

Some people can speak with such confidence to the extent that they can mask the topic. The things that they talk about sound correct simply because they know how to express themselves. They may not know much about the particular thing that they're talking about. However, they talk because all this information is stored within and they don't need to access and reprocess this. Perhaps it's an area that they're so confident about that they don't need to try to process information constantly. It may be an area that they spend time on quite regularly.

Take a teacher, a professor, or lecturer, for example. Because they're constantly speaking on a topic, they may find that they don't have to constantly look at what they're talking about. They may not need to add more information because they're simply regurgitating or repeating the same information over and over. They appear to share information that's simply there.

When we start processing information is when we start accessing the information and commence speaking about it. This is when we start sharing it or start accessing it in such a way that we can truly acknowledge it. Because we act on those packets of information that are in our brain, that is when we realise that we do know more than we think we know.

HOW MUCH DO YOU REALLY KNOW?

I recently had a conversation with a colleague and I was actually seeking help. When I asked for that help, he said to me, "I know nothing." I chuckled, then considered this reply for a while and realised maybe he was right. What do we really know?

Knowledge in itself is merely a bunch of information and data, all put together for some usage that could be positive or negative. It becomes power when you put it into action. So, as you gather all this information, it's only data collected. If you don't put it together to make sense to yourself or to someone else, it's really not something that you know.

The next time you pick up a newspaper or a magazine and you read through it, realise that only reading through materials or browsing through them does not automatically mean you will retain anything. You may not gain any kind of particular knowledge. It's similar to you sitting and allowing the breeze to merely pass you by. You may smell, feel, and remain in that position or state in which you were before that moment or the momentary experience that you probably just missed.

Unless we process information that we gather, we may realise at some point that we have not gained anything. We did not actually retain much, hence we're not able to share much. One mentor clarified this with me once, saying: "Andrew, remember, if you're not reading, you don't have anything to share. If you're not gaining additional information, you're not able to share valuable information or make much impact."

Today, I urge you to re-examine the things that you think you know and especially your obsession with the stuff that is going on around our day-to-day life. Re-examine what you think you really know and what you really feel confident about. Why not take the time out to ask yourself, "What do I really know?"

KNOW AND GO

Once we know that we are confident and we are pleased, then we should be happy to make that next step. We only need to take action. Take one step forward and you can literally imagine in your head, and in your psyche, that you are about to take that leap forward. Whether it be a jump, a dive, or a footstep. Whether you want to crawl, or whether you want to simply reach out or reach up. Move in a forward motion. Make a simple act today. Maintaining this action will propel you toward great, unimaginable heights.

Once you know, once you've made a choice that, "I will do this!" or "I am ready!" you do not have to worry about what you need. Take what you have right now, at this moment. Know that what you know within yourself is useful. Take that one step or that leap in a consistent direction and go.

If it's only little by little, that one step maintained consistently will eventually grow into a collective of movements and of actions taken. As shared in my journey, it is in moving forward that you can look back and see the progress that you are making. It is in going that you can review. It is in knowing and going collectively that you can actually measure the progress that you have accomplished or that you can alter on your journey.

KNOWING IS HALF THE BATTLE

We become knowledgeable when we take the time out to access and process information and when we use the information that we've gathered, whether through listening, reading, writing, or observation. We are able to consider ourselves as better off than we were if we had not gathered anything new or processed any new form of information.

I can think back to my childhood and, more recently, to a film, *G.I. Joe*. They had this constant saying: "Knowing is half the battle." I believe that in knowing, and particularly in processing information that we have gathered, we are actually able to stand out. We are able to command. We are able to take a lead, and most times, take a step away from the negative and the stagnation and the urge of the downward spiral feelings. We can change that path that we are on in a more positive manner.

In knowing—and particularly, this includes actually writing down our destination, our goals, or aims that we're trying to achieve—we can take a leap and the lead. In knowing that which we are trying to achieve, we can often take charge once we at least take action toward our goals and our aspirations. We can spark an interest in ourselves and in other people. We also process some goals toward our next step.

It may be your second step or third. However, merely by taking that next step and acting on the information you have now processed, you are actually in a state of motion. You would have now taken another step in the stages from where you once were. You would now find yourself in a better position, a better state.

KNOWLEDGE & PASSION

Passion is necessary and it's also natural. You develop passion for what you want and what you want to do. Through a natural means of internal energy, it drives you to do whatever it takes. This internal energy is emitted through emotions and strong desire. Passion is a driving force and when it is developed within you, you almost become unstoppable. With passion and knowing the right people, knowing the right things, and having some knowledge in your area of interest, you grow in an exponential manner.

When you like something and develop a passion for it, you feel, you think, and you imagine. You get closer to it psychologically. The liking for that thing may evolve into love and sometimes, an obsession. This is how dangerous or serious passion advances. Your love may be more intimate. You become more emotionally attached and you feel more in tune with that thing you initially liked. When it comes to you achieving success, reaching your aim, or meeting your goal, knowing even a little is impactful. Knowing what you want to do and knowing about what you're seeking, emits energy. This ignites what you thought was not there.

Being passionate builds energy on top of what you know and the little that you know is all you need. As with passion, embracing the little knowledge you have may inspire you. You become a powerful force to be reckoned with. Coupled with action, it is almost like when two elements collide and create a supernatural, super-power force.

This is what the energy and passion creates. It embraces you. It picks you up and it puts you into motion status. I simply ask you to take that one step. Take that one leap forward or upward. Move and let these two driving elements take you through to the end—all the way through to the end result, your achievement. Then, when you are reflecting, you realise that you know more than you actually think you know.

SUCCESS AND KNOWLEDGE

There is no doubt that to become successful, there are some things you must know and that you need to know. There are some people whom you need to know and need to access. There are some things that you may not want to do, but because you want success, you need to do these simple, little, and sometimes insignificant things.

Simple things like knowing what you want to achieve, knowing what you are seeking, and knowing why you want to achieve it. Know why you want to have this success. Only you can do this. Only you can know what you want and how you want it to look, feel, or be. But you must have an idea. By knowing this little bit and by accessing someone with the right knowledge, you are on the way to become successful.

Many times, I will speak to a leader or, at least, a leader in their own field. Someone who has achieved a level of success or who has acted on their achievement of success. The same things pop up. They will insist that you must have a mentor, you must be coachable, and you need some sort of guidance. This is where knowing the right person becomes effective.

Choosing the right person to work with may be dependent on what you know or who you know. And you don't have to become all knowledgeable in your field. You simply need to take action. Take action with the little knowledge you have to reach out, seek help, and seek the right guidance.

And it is my hope that with the Knowledge Cube, it is and will be simpler for you to meet with someone and for you to access some level of support and to be guided. For you to have someone to whom you can be accountable to achieve success with your own intentions, with your own goals in mind, and with the little knowledge you have developing.

With your success journey, when you act on this knowledge, you're on the way to becoming an expert in your field and becoming more successful—and to be an example among your peers, friends, and family. This little knowledge you have and act upon becomes yours for you to keep as you become more and more successful.

THE KNOWLEDGE YOU NEED TO FLOW

Knowledge is power, or so they say. I would say knowledge acted upon is that power which you need to propel yourself forward, upward, ahead of the game, and onto the right path to success, on track to your progression. The knowledge you need to flow is often accessible within you. Perhaps you need to access this knowledge or collection of data, but definitely, you already have this knowledge that you need within you.

This is made up of different elements. It could be your friend or an associate who has similar objectives. Someone who has your interests at heart and who knows about your aspirations. They are willing to support you or are already supporting you. It could be a family member who calls themselves a team member. Perhaps someone who happens to energise you, encourages you, and is supporting you. It could be husband or wife or a significant other. It could be your kids. It could even be you being capable of working in a group or as a team. Perhaps you work in such a way where it does not affect others negatively.

As you use your collection of data, the ideas, and the information and reorder them, you will restructure them. By directing your energies in one specific direction, your knowledge, acted upon, becomes that knowledge you need to flow.

As was highlighted in the Knowledge Cube explained in the previous chapters, only you can give that nudge that drives you forward. Perhaps you do not realise it. You can be poked, you can be waved at, and others can cheer you on. You can be motivated through others. You can be encouraged in such a way that the only thing left to do is to be inspired and act on the knowledge you need to flow

Until you make that leap, until you use your own energies and your own ideas, until you make that final decision, that choice, until you make that unintentional or minor step or action, the knowledge you need to flow remains with you.

REFLECTIVE NOTES

Identify one message I received from this chapter:

How does this make me feel?

Who will I speak with to assist me?

What actions can I take right now?

Go to – **www.TheKnowledgeCube.info**—*to discover more*

"You

Know

More

Than

You

Think

You

Know"

Go to – **www.TheKnowledgeCube.info—***to discover more*

48668546R00074

Printed in Poland
by Amazon Fulfillment
Poland Sp. z o.o., Wrocław